Multiply your Arithmetic skills with CGP!

The best way to prepare for the KS2 SATs Arithmetic paper is to practise as much as possible... and that's where this brilliant CGP book comes in!

It's packed with questions for every Arithmetic topic, in the style of the real SATs. All the answers are included and there's a progress chart, so it's easy to mark your work and see how you're getting on.

And to help you get used to dealing with a range of topics, there's a practice test at the end of the book. It's a perfect warm-up for the real thing!

What CGP is all about

Our sole aim here at CGP is to produce the highest quality books
— carefully written, immaculately presented and
dangerously close to being funny.

Then we work our socks off to get them out to you
— at the cheapest possible prices.

Contents

Section One — Whole Numbers

Place Value 2

Negative Numbers 3

Square and Cube Numbers 5

Order of Operations 6

Mixed Practice 8

Section Two — Calculations

Written Addition 10

Written Subtraction 13

Multiplying and Dividing by 10, 100 and 1000 16

Using Times Tables 18

Written Multiplication 20

Written Division 24

Mixed Practice 28

Section Three — Decimals

Adding and Subtracting Decimals 30

Multiplying and Dividing by 10, 100 and 1000 32

Multiplying with Decimals 34

Dividing with Decimals 36

Mixed Practice 38

Section Four — Fractions

Adding and Subtracting Fractions 40

Multiplying Fractions 43

Dividing Fractions 45

Percentages 46

Mixed Practice 48

Practice Test 50

Answers 55

Progress Chart 62

Published by CGP

Editors: Ruth Greenhalgh, Samuel Mann, Tom Miles

With thanks to Alison Griffin, Simon Little
and Dave Ryan for the proofreading.
Also thanks to Jan Greenway for the copyright research.

*Contains public sector information licensed under the
Open Government Licence v3.0.
http://www.nationalarchives.gov.uk/doc/open-
government-licence/version/3/*

ISBN: 978 1 78908 614 0

Printed by Bell & Bain Ltd, Glasgow.
Clipart from Corel®

Based on the classic CGP style created by Richard Parsons.

Text, design, layout and original illustrations
© Coordination Group Publications Ltd. (CGP) 2020
All rights reserved.

**Photocopying this book is not permitted, even if you have a CLA licence.
Extra copies are available from CGP with next day delivery • 0800 1712 712 • www.cgpbooks.co.uk**

Section One — Whole Numbers

Place Value

1) Work out:

396 + 10

672 − 100

2 marks

2) Fill in the boxes with the correct numbers.

46 521 = 40 000 + ☐ + 500 + 20 + 1

870 310 = 800 000 + 70 000 + ☐ + 10

2 marks

3) Calculate:

632 + 1000

1000 + 9857

2 marks

4) Find the missing numbers.

? − 10 = 197

? + 100 = 5044

2 marks

"I can find 10, 100 and 1000 more or less than any number and can work out the value of each digit."

Negative Numbers

Use the number line below to help you with the questions on these pages.

1 Work out:

0 – 7

0 – 13

2 marks

2 Find the answers to the calculations below.

–5 + 4 =

–7 + 3 =

2 marks

–9 + 9 =

–11 + 6 =

2 marks

3 Calculate:

–3 – 2

–6 – 1

2 marks

–10 – 9

–8 – 7

2 marks

Negative Numbers

4 Work out:

8 − 9

12 − 15

2 marks

5 Fill in the missing numbers to make these calculations correct.

☐ = −4 + 6

☐ = −7 + 10

2 marks

☐ + 15 = 6

☐ + 14 = 3

2 marks

6 Work out the answers to these calculations.

5 − 45

−84 − 7

2 marks

−36 − 44

−52 + 68

2 marks

"I can calculate using negative numbers."

Square and Cube Numbers

1 Work out:

$2^2 = $

$1^2 = $

$6^2 = $

2 marks

$11^2 = $

2 marks

2 Calculate:

$3^3 = $

$5^3 = $

$0^3 = $

2 marks

$10^3 = $

2 marks

3 Fill in the boxes with the correct numbers.

$\boxed{}^2 = 16$

$\boxed{}^3 = 8$

2 marks

4 Find the answers to these calculations.

$12^2 - 1$

$1^3 + 100$

2 marks

"I can use square and cube numbers in calculations."

Order of Operations

1) Find the answers to these calculations.

24 ÷ 6 + 2

12 × 5 − 3

2 marks

2) Calculate:

70 + (3 × 4)

35 − (50 ÷ 2)

2 marks

3) Work out:

6 × (18 − 15)

(54 + 27) ÷ 9

2 marks

4) Work out the answers to these calculations.

48 − 32 ÷ 8

70 + 10 × 7

2 marks

Order of Operations

5) Work out:

$90 - 9^2$ 7×2^3

   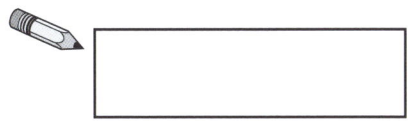

2 marks

$2^2 + 3^2$ $8^2 - 1^3$

2 marks

6) Calculate:

$7^2 + 8 \times 6$ $3^3 - 18 \div 9$

2 marks

7) Work out the answers to the calculations below.

$(5 + 3)^2 \div 16$ $5^3 \times (4 - 1)$

2 marks

"I know the order to do things in a calculation."

Mixed Practice

That's the end of Whole Numbers — test how much you've learnt with these questions.

1 Calculate:

9924 + 1000

2056 − 100

2 marks

2 Fill in the boxes to partition these numbers.

795 016 = 700 000 + 90 000 + ☐ + 10 + 6

☐ = 100 000 + 80 000 + 2000 + 70

☐ = 600 000 + 9000 + 900 + 30 + 5

3 marks

3 Find the missing numbers to make these calculations correct.

☐ = 7 − 13

☐ = −8 + 80

2 marks

4 Work out:

4^2 = ☐

4^3 = ☐

2 marks

Section One — Whole Numbers

Mixed Practice

5) Find the answers to these calculations.

9 × (10 − 5)   24 + 36 ÷ 12

2 marks

6) Work out the answers to the calculations below.

100 − 5²   10² + 10³

2 marks

7) Calculate:

45 − 100   −85 + 92

2 marks

8) Find the answers to these calculations.

(3³ + 2) × 10   2 × 70 − 8²

2 marks

Check how well you've done with Whole Numbers by adding up your marks from these Mixed Practice pages. Write your score in the box on the right, then fill in the scoresheet at the end of the book.

/ 17

Section Two — Calculations

Written Addition

1) Calculate:

126 + 504 =

1 mark

497 + 203 =

1 mark

2) Work out:

452 + 241   7041 + 357

2 marks

3) Fill in the missing numbers to make these calculations correct.

☐ = 33 + 751

1 mark

☐ = 571 + 305

1 mark

☐ = 686 + 282

1 mark

Written Addition

4 Find the answer to:

986 + 745

8736 + 637

2 marks

5 Work out the answers to these calculations.

2305 + 3416 =

1 mark

5933 + 1325 =

1 mark

8542 + 7235 =

1 mark

6 Calculate:

3823 + 1299

49 285 + 1631

2 marks

Written Addition

7 Work out 8300 + 68 700.

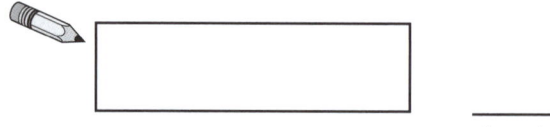
1 mark

8 Calculate:

36 752 + 6285   54 906 + 81 347

   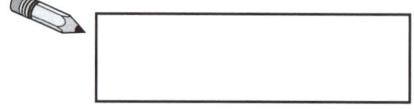
2 marks

9 Find the answer to the calculation below.

759 218 + 85 945

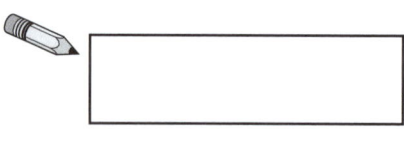
1 mark

"I can use standard written methods to add whole numbers."

Written Subtraction

1 Work out:

458 − 101 = ☐

1 mark

715 − 306 = ☐

1 mark

1672 − 49 = ☐

1 mark

2 Find the answers to these calculations.

4000 − 30

70 000 − 600

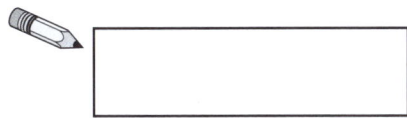

2 marks

3 Calculate:

735 − 268

2614 − 943

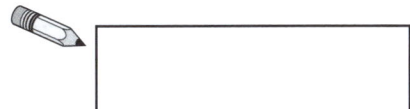

2 marks

Written Subtraction

4 Fill in the missing numbers to make these calculations correct.

 = 357 − 324

1 mark

 = 528 − 83

1 mark

 = 671 − 412

1 mark

5 What number is missing from this calculation?

822 − ? = 185

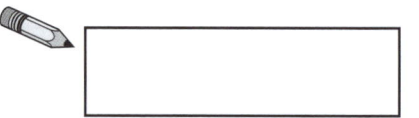

1 mark

6 Work out:

8284 − 1348   9091 − 2799

2 marks

Written Subtraction

7 Work out the number missing from the subtraction below.

64 110 − [ ] = 237

1 mark

8 Work out:

72 559 − 28 667   46 485 − 26 898

2 marks

9 Find the answer to the calculation below.

909 145 − 89 152

1 mark

"I can use standard written methods to subtract whole numbers."

Multiplying and Dividing by 10, 100 and 1000

1 Calculate:

41 × 10

57 × 100

2 marks

2 Work out:

80 ÷ 10

300 ÷ 100

2 marks

3 Fill in the missing numbers.

676 × 100 =

1 mark

93 × 10 × 10 =

1 mark

5 × 10 × 100 =

1 mark

4 Work out:

500 ÷ 10

72 000 ÷ 10

2 marks

Multiplying and Dividing by 10, 100 and 1000

5 Calculate:

36 × 1000

8000 ÷ 1000

2 marks

6 Work out the answers to these multiplications.

535 × 1000

2793 × 100

2 marks

7 Work out the answers to these divisions.

38 000 ÷ 1000

60 000 ÷ 1000

2 marks

8 Find the missing numbers in these calculations.

4900 ÷ ☐ = 490

1 mark

57 × 10 × ☐ = 57 000

1 mark

"I can multiply and divide whole numbers by 10, 100 and 1000."

Using Times Tables

1 Give the answers to these times table multiplications.

7 × 9

11 × 12

2 marks

2 Work out:

32 ÷ 8

84 ÷ 7

2 marks

3 Find the missing numbers in these calculations.

6 × ? = 42

121 ÷ ? = 11

2 marks

4 Calculate:

2 × 3 × 9

4 × 5 × 10

2 marks

Using Times Tables

5 What numbers are missing from these calculations?

81 ×  = 0

27 ÷  = 27

2 marks

6 Work out the answers to these multiplications.

50 × 60

80 × 30

2 marks

7 Work out the answers to these divisions.

350 ÷ 7

490 ÷ 70

2 marks

8 Work out:

4 × 3 × 60

20 × 30 × 8

2 marks

"I can multiply and divide numbers mentally using known facts."

Written Multiplication

1 Work out the calculations below.

4 × 52

34 × 3

2 marks

2 Multiply these numbers together.

28 × 5

7 × 49

2 marks

3 Calculate:

226 × 3

8 × 306

2 marks

Written Multiplication

4 Work out:

495 × 6

798 × 9

2 marks

5 Work out the answers to these multiplications.

1071 × 5

2489 × 3

2 marks

6 Use long multiplication to multiply these numbers.

```
   2 3
 × 1 3
 -----
```

```
   3 1
 × 1 6
 -----
```

4 marks

Written Multiplication

7 Multiply these numbers together.

4 marks

8 Work out the answers to these multiplications.

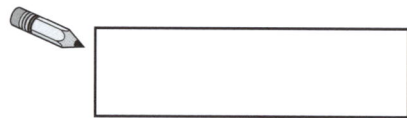

4 marks

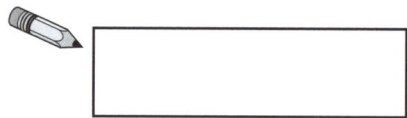

4 marks

Written Multiplication

9 Work out:

4 marks

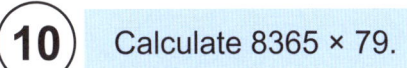

4 marks

10 Calculate 8365 × 79.

2 marks

"I can multiply a four-digit number by a two-digit number."

Written Division

1 Calculate:

72 ÷ 3   98 ÷ 7

2 marks

2 Work out:

436 ÷ 4   558 ÷ 6

   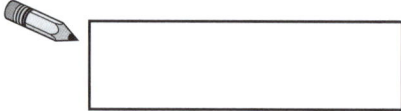

2 marks

3 Use short division to find the answers to these calculations.

8968 ÷ 8   4285 ÷ 5

2 marks

Written Division

4 Do these short divisions, giving the remainder as a whole number.

76 ÷ 3   291 ÷ 9

   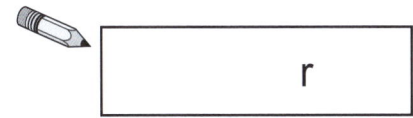

r   r

2 marks

5 Work out these divisions, giving the remainder as a whole number.

9704 ÷ 6   4199 ÷ 8

   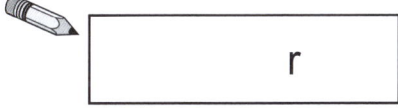

r   r

2 marks

6 Use a written method to do these calculations.

13 ⟌ 1 9 5   21 ⟌ 2 5 2

   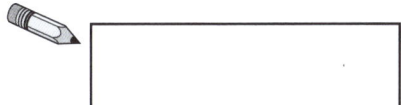

4 marks

© CGP — Not to be photocopied   Section Two — Calculations

Written Division

7 Do these divisions using a written method.

$24\overline{)528}$ $\qquad\qquad\qquad$ $33\overline{)825}$

4 marks

8 Find the answers to these calculations using a written method.

$43\overline{)5246}$ $\qquad\qquad\qquad$ $74\overline{)9176}$

4 marks

$52\overline{)4888}$ $\qquad\qquad\qquad$ $39\overline{)3705}$

4 marks

Section Two — Calculations

Written Division

9 Do these divisions, giving the remainder as a whole number.

[   ] r [ ]   [   ] r [ ]

4 marks

10 Work out these divisions, giving the remainder as a whole number.

[   ] r [ ]   [   ] r [ ]

4 marks

"I can divide a four-digit number by a two-digit number."

Mixed Practice

That's the end of Calculations — test how much you've learnt with these questions.

1 Work out:

54 × 100

604 × 1000

2 marks

7800 ÷ 10

42 000 ÷ 100

2 marks

2 Find the answers to these calculations.

☐ = 881 + 419

1 mark

☐ = 796 − 378

1 mark

9831 − ☐ = 251

1 mark

3 Calculate:

3 × 3 × 8

50 × 2 × 4

2 marks

Mixed Practice

4 Work out the answers to these calculations.

3668 ÷ 4   9036 × 7

   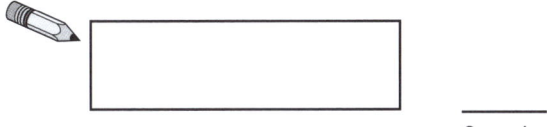

2 marks

5 Calculate:

793 568 + 27 384   503 614 − 84 789

   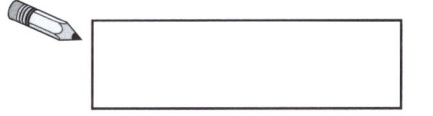

2 marks

6 Work out each of the calculations below.

$$\begin{array}{r} 9723 \\ \times 84 \\ \hline \end{array}$$ 67) 6164

4 marks

Check how well you've done with Calculations by adding up your marks from these Mixed Practice pages. Write your score in the box on the right, then fill in the scoresheet at the end of the book.   / 17

Adding and Subtracting Decimals

1 Work out:

4.3 + 5.6 = ☐

7.6 − 0.2 = ☐

2 marks

35.8 + 2.5 = ☐

69.4 − 4.7 = ☐

2 marks

2 Find the answers to these calculations:

2.86 + 3.61

25.09 − 1.34

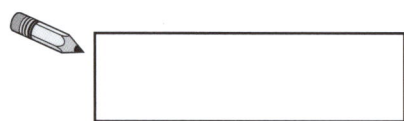

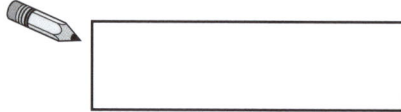

2 marks

3 Calculate:

116.74 + 42.4

8.27 − 5.4

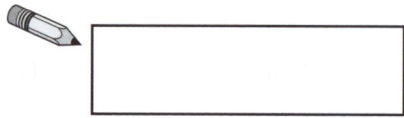

2 marks

Adding and Subtracting Decimals

4 Find:

12.641 − 4.39

6.3 + 7.842

2 marks

5 Find the answers to these subtractions:

8 − 2.7

34.3 − 16.52

2 marks

6 Work out:

326.52 + 74.9

23.6 − 7.814

2 marks

"I can add and subtract decimal numbers."

Multiplying and Dividing by 10, 100 and 1000

1 Find the answers to these calculations:

13.2 × 10 =

1 mark

9.431 × 10 =

1 mark

204.78 × 10 =

1 mark

2 Work out:

3.15 × 100   62.8 × 100

2 marks

3 Calculate:

4.87 × 1000 =

1 mark

6.935 × 1000 =

1 mark

124.3 × 1000 =

1 mark

4 Find:

0.8 ÷ 10   1.63 ÷ 10

2 marks

Section Three — Decimals   © CGP — Not to be photocopied

Multiplying and Dividing by 10, 100 and 1000

5 Work out the answers to these calculations:

0.6 ÷ 100

17 ÷ 100

2 marks

2.8 ÷ 100

24.6 ÷ 100

2 marks

6 Calculate:

349 ÷ 1000

12 ÷ 1000

2 marks

7 Fill in the boxes with the correct numbers.

7.486 × ☐ = 748.6

1 mark

☐ ÷ 10 = 0.01

1 mark

3075 ÷ ☐ = 3.075

1 mark

"I can multiply and divide decimal numbers by 10, 100 and 1000."

Multiplying with Decimals

1) Calculate:

0.5 × 6 = ☐   0.04 × 9 = ☐

2 marks

3 × 0.08 = ☐   11 × 0.7 = ☐

2 marks

2) Find the answers to these multiplications:

0.6 × 80 = ☐

1 mark

0.02 × 50 = ☐

1 mark

300 × 0.07 = ☐

1 mark

3) Work out:

5.2 × 4   27 × 0.8

☐   ☐

2 marks

Section Three — Decimals   © CGP — Not to be photocopied

Multiplying with Decimals

4 Find:

0.06 × 35

6.41 × 7

2 marks

5 Work out:

2.9 × 40

5.37 × 50

2 marks

6 Calculate:

3.4 × 15

25 × 9.2

4 marks

"I can multiply decimal numbers by whole numbers."

Dividing with Decimals

1 Work out the answers to these divisions:

0.8 ÷ 4 =

3.2 ÷ 8 =

2 marks

0.56 ÷ 7 =

8.4 ÷ 12 =

2 marks

2 Find:

6.9 ÷ 3 =

1 mark

4.82 ÷ 2 =

1 mark

15.5 ÷ 5 =

1 mark

3 Work out:

25.6 ÷ 8

1.08 ÷ 4

2 marks

Dividing with Decimals

4) Work out these divisions, giving your answer as a decimal.

12 ÷ 5   43 ÷ 4

2 marks

5) Write the answers to these divisions as decimals:

159 ÷ 6   426 ÷ 8

2 marks

6) Find the answers to these divisions. Give your answers as decimals.

22 ⟌ 4 7 3   12 ⟌ 5 2 1 4

4 marks

"I can use standard written methods to do divisions involving decimal numbers."

Mixed Practice

That's the end of Decimals — test how much you've learnt with these questions.

1) Find the answers to these sums:

4.19 + 3.25

7.53 + 2.648

2 marks

2) Work out:

8.97 × 10 =

0.62 × 1000 =

2 marks

0.3 ÷ 100 =

58 ÷ 1000 =

2 marks

3) Calculate:

25.3 − 16.7

9 − 7.29

2 marks

Mixed Practice

4) Work out:

0.05 × 7 = ☐   0.36 ÷ 9 = ☐

2 marks

5) Find the answers to these multiplications.

8.42 × 5   44 × 5.4

☐   ☐

3 marks

6) Write the answers to these divisions as decimals:

3.78 ÷ 6   329 ÷ 14

☐   ☐

3 marks

Check how well you've done with Decimals by adding up your marks from these Mixed Practice pages. Write your score in the box on the right, then fill in the scoresheet at the end of the book.

/ 16

Section Three — Decimals

Section Four — Fractions

Adding and Subtracting Fractions

1 Calculate:

$\frac{3}{7} + \frac{2}{7}$

$\frac{5}{8} + \frac{4}{8}$

2 marks

2 Work out:

$\frac{7}{9} - \frac{1}{9}$

$\frac{9}{12} - \frac{5}{12}$

2 marks

3 Find the answer to each of these calculations.

$\frac{4}{5} + \frac{2}{15}$

$\frac{1}{2} - \frac{1}{6}$

2 marks

$\frac{5}{6} + \frac{8}{9}$

$\frac{11}{16} - \frac{3}{12}$

2 marks

Adding and Subtracting Fractions

4 Fill in the boxes.

$1\frac{2}{5} + \frac{3}{5} =$ ☐

$1\frac{1}{10} - \frac{3}{10} =$ ☐

2 marks

5 What are the answers to these sums?

$\frac{2}{11} + \frac{5}{11} + \frac{1}{11}$

$\frac{5}{14} + \frac{1}{7} + \frac{2}{14}$

2 marks

6 Work out:

$\frac{3}{5} + \frac{1}{4}$

$\frac{2}{6} + \frac{2}{7}$

2 marks

$\frac{9}{10} - \frac{2}{3}$

$\frac{6}{11} - \frac{1}{2}$

2 marks

Adding and Subtracting Fractions

7 Calculate the answers to:

$5\frac{3}{8} + \frac{3}{4}$

$2\frac{2}{3} - \frac{4}{5}$

8 Find the answer to each of these calculations.

$1\frac{1}{4} + 1\frac{1}{3}$

$2\frac{1}{6} - 1\frac{2}{5}$

"I can add and subtract fractions by finding a common denominator."

Multiplying Fractions

1) What is:

$\dfrac{1}{4}$ of 400?

$\dfrac{2}{5}$ of 1000?

2 marks

2) Find the answers to these calculations.

$\dfrac{1}{9} \times 270 =$

1 mark

$\dfrac{1}{6} \times 6600 =$

1 mark

3) Work out:

$\dfrac{5}{7} \times 14$

$\dfrac{51}{100} \times 200$

2 marks

4) Find:

$\dfrac{2}{3}$ of 210

$\dfrac{3}{4}$ of 30

2 marks

Multiplying Fractions

5 Work out the answers to these multiplications.

$1\frac{1}{2} \times 32$

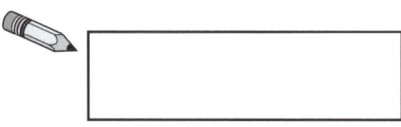
1 mark

$1\frac{2}{5} \times 125$

1 mark

6 Calculate:

$\frac{1}{5} \times \frac{1}{11}$ $\frac{1}{2} \times \frac{3}{8}$

2 marks

$\frac{9}{10} \times \frac{2}{3}$ $\frac{3}{4} \times \frac{2}{15}$

2 marks

"I can multiply fractions by whole numbers and by other fractions."

Dividing Fractions

1 Calculate:

$\dfrac{7}{10} \div 7$ $\qquad\qquad\qquad\qquad$ $\dfrac{2}{3} \div 2$

2 marks

$\dfrac{8}{13} \div 4$ $\qquad\qquad\qquad\qquad$ $\dfrac{20}{75} \div 10$

2 marks

2 Work out:

$\dfrac{1}{3} \div 4$ $\qquad\qquad\qquad\qquad$ $\dfrac{1}{6} \div 10$

2 marks

$\dfrac{3}{8} \div 5$ $\qquad\qquad\qquad\qquad$ $\dfrac{2}{7} \div 4$

2 marks

"I can divide fractions by whole numbers."

Percentages

1 Fill in the boxes.

10% of 500 = [ ]

1 mark

25% of 4000 = [ ]

1 mark

50% of 840 = [ ]

1 mark

1% of 1000 = [ ]

1 mark

2 Work out:

20% of 120

60% of 3600

[ ]   [ ]

2 marks

15% of 940

65% of 280

[ ]   [ ]

2 marks

Percentages

3 Calculate:

40% × 10 000   35% × 160

2 marks

4 Find these percentages.

99% of 4500   49% of 700

   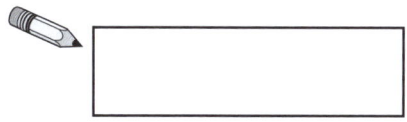

2 marks

9% of 300   26% of 600

   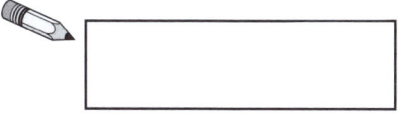

2 marks

5 Work out:

67% of 1600

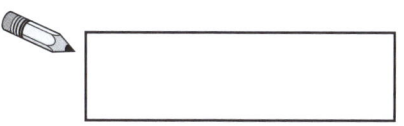

1 mark

"I can find a percentage of an amount."

Mixed Practice

That's the end of Fractions — test how much you've learnt with these questions.

1 Find:

30% × 270

90% × 5000

2 marks

2 Work out the answers to these multiplications.

$\frac{1}{8} \times 560$

$\frac{2}{5} \times 450$

2 marks

3 Work out:

$\frac{1}{10} + \frac{2}{9}$

$\frac{1}{2} - \frac{3}{7}$

2 marks

4 What is 52% of 2800?

1 mark

Section Four — Fractions

Mixed Practice

5 Find:

$\frac{4}{5} \div 10$

$\frac{1}{9} \div 3$

2 marks

6 Work out $\frac{5}{6} \times \frac{4}{5}$.

1 mark

7 Calculate:

$1\frac{3}{5} + \frac{2}{3}$

1 mark

$1\frac{5}{6} - \frac{9}{12}$

1 mark

$1\frac{1}{3} \times 90$

1 mark

Check how well you've done with Fractions by adding up your marks from these Mixed Practice pages. Write your score in the box on the right, then fill in the scoresheet at the end of the book.

/ 13

Practice Test

1 Fill in the missing number to make this calculation correct.

☐ = 5918 + 1000

1 mark

2 Calculate 1653 − 262.

☐

1 mark

3 Find the missing number.

☐ + 10 = 509

1 mark

4 Work out 66 ÷ 6.

☐

1 mark

5 Work out:

☐ = 675 × 0

1 mark

6 Fill in the missing number.

☐ = 28 × 100

1 mark

7 Calculate 4275 + 376.

☐

1 mark

8 Find the missing number.

21.4 − 5.3 = ☐

1 mark

9 Work out 37 × 6.

☐

1 mark

10 Fill in the missing number to make this calculation correct.

☐ = 720 ÷ 12

1 mark

11 Work out:

59 000 ÷ 100 = ☐

1 mark

12 Find the missing number.

82.5 + 7.68 = ☐

1 mark

13 Fill in the box to partition this number.

302 178 = 300 000 + ☐ + 100 + 70 + 8

1 mark

14 Calculate 25 049 − 6158.

☐

1 mark

15 Find the answers to these divisions:

336 ÷ 8   756 ÷ 6

2 marks

16 Find the answer to $7^2 - 50$.

1 mark

17 Fill in the missing number.

☐ = 41.27 × 100

1 mark

18 Work out:

$\frac{1}{3}$ of 9300 $\frac{3}{10}$ of 620

2 marks

19 Calculate $\frac{7}{12} + \frac{7}{8}$.

1 mark

20 Calculate:

40 × (50 + 20) = ☐

1 mark

21 Find the missing number.

942 ÷ ☐ = 0.942

1 mark

22 Work out $2\frac{1}{5} - 1\frac{5}{9}$.

1 mark

23 Find the answers to these multiplications:

```
  6 5 4
×   3 4
```

```
  8 2 1 6
×     4 7
```

4 marks

24 $\frac{16}{17} \div 4 =$

1 mark

25 Calculate 18 − 7.926.

1 mark

26 What is 78% × 1200?

1 mark

27 Work out:

4 × 7.2   50 × 3.4

2 marks

28 Find the answer to these calculations.

$\frac{19}{20} \div 3$ $\frac{3}{7} \times \frac{5}{8}$

2 marks

29 $2\frac{7}{9} \times 18 =$

1 mark

30 Find the answers to these calculations using a written method.

34) 7 8 2   56) 5 2 0 8

4 marks

Check how well you've done by adding up your marks from this Practice Test. Write your score in the box on the right, then fill in the scoresheet at the end of the book.

/ 40

Answers

Section One — Whole Numbers

Page 2 — Place Value

1) 396 + 10 = **406** *(1 mark)*
   672 − 100 = **572** *(1 mark)*

2) 46 521 = 40 000 + **6000** + 500 + 20 + 1 *(1 mark)*
   870 310 = 800 000 + 70 000 + **300** + 10 *(1 mark)*

3) 632 + 1000 = **1632** *(1 mark)*
   1000 + 9857 = **10 857** *(1 mark)*

4) **207** − 10 = 197 *(1 mark)*
   4944 + 100 = 5044 *(1 mark)*

Pages 3-4 — Negative Numbers

1) 0 − 7 = **−7** *(1 mark)*
   0 − 13 = **−13** *(1 mark)*

2) −5 + 4 = **−1** *(1 mark)*
   −7 + 3 = **−4** *(1 mark)*
   −9 + 9 = **0** *(1 mark)*
   −11 + 6 = **−5** *(1 mark)*

3) −3 − 2 = **−5** *(1 mark)*
   −6 − 1 = **−7** *(1 mark)*
   −10 − 9 = **−19** *(1 mark)*
   −8 − 7 = **−15** *(1 mark)*

4) 8 − 9 = **−1** *(1 mark)*
   12 − 15 = **−3** *(1 mark)*

5) **2** = −4 + 6 *(1 mark)*
   3 = −7 + 10 *(1 mark)*
   −9 + 15 = 6 *(1 mark)*
   −11 + 14 = 3 *(1 mark)*

6) 5 − 45 = **−40** *(1 mark)*
   −84 − 7 = **−91** *(1 mark)*
   −36 − 44 = **−80** *(1 mark)*
   −52 + 68 = **16** *(1 mark)*

Page 5 — Square and Cube Numbers

1) $2^2 = 2 \times 2 = $ **4** *(1 mark)*
   $6^2 = 6 \times 6 = $ **36** *(1 mark)*
   $1^2 = 1 \times 1 = $ **1** *(1 mark)*
   $11^2 = 11 \times 11 = $ **121** *(1 mark)*

2) $3^3 = 3 \times 3 \times 3 = $ **27** *(1 mark)*
   $0^3 = 0 \times 0 \times 0 = $ **0** *(1 mark)*
   $5^3 = 5 \times 5 \times 5 = $ **125** *(1 mark)*
   $10^3 = 10 \times 10 \times 10 = $ **1000** *(1 mark)*

3) $\mathbf{4}^2 = 4 \times 4 = 16$ *(1 mark)*
   $\mathbf{2}^3 = 2 \times 2 \times 2 = 8$ *(1 mark)*

4) $12^2 − 1 = 144 − 1 = $ **143** *(1 mark)*
   $1^3 + 100 = 1 + 100 = $ **101** *(1 mark)*

Pages 6-7 — Order of Operations

1) 24 ÷ 6 + 2 = 4 + 2 = **6** *(1 mark)*
   12 × 5 − 3 = 60 − 3 = **57** *(1 mark)*

2) 70 + (3 × 4) = 70 + 12 = **82** *(1 mark)*
   35 − (50 ÷ 2) = 35 − 25 = **10** *(1 mark)*

3) 6 × (18 − 15) = 6 × 3 = **18** *(1 mark)*
   (54 + 27) ÷ 9 = 81 ÷ 9 = **9** *(1 mark)*

4) 48 − 32 ÷ 8 = 48 − 4 = **44** *(1 mark)*
   70 + 10 × 7 = 70 + 70 = **140** *(1 mark)*

5) $90 − 9^2 = 90 − 81 = $ **9** *(1 mark)*
   $7 \times 2^3 = 7 \times 8 = $ **56** *(1 mark)*
   $2^2 + 3^2 = 4 + 9 = $ **13** *(1 mark)*
   $8^2 − 1^3 = 64 − 1 = $ **63** *(1 mark)*

6) $7^2 + 8 \times 6 = 49 + 48 = $ **97** *(1 mark)*
   $3^3 − 18 ÷ 9 = 27 − 2 = $ **25** *(1 mark)*

7) $(5 + 3)^2 ÷ 16 = 8^2 ÷ 16 = 64 ÷ 16 = $ **4** *(1 mark)*
   $5^3 \times (4 − 1) = 125 \times 3 = $ **375** *(1 mark)*

Pages 8-9 — Mixed Practice

1) 9924 + 1000 = **10 924** *(1 mark)*
   2056 − 100 = **1956** *(1 mark)*

2) 795 016 = 700 000 + 90 000 + **5000** + 10 + 6 *(1 mark)*
   182 070 = 100 000 + 80 000 + 2000 + 70 *(1 mark)*
   609 935 = 600 000 + 9000 + 900 + 30 + 5 *(1 mark)*

3) **−6** = 7 − 13 *(1 mark)*
   72 = −8 + 80 *(1 mark)*

4) $4^2 = 4 \times 4 = $ **16** *(1 mark)*
   $4^3 = 4 \times 4 \times 4 = $ **64** *(1 mark)*

5) 9 × (10 − 5) = 9 × 5 = **45** *(1 mark)*
   24 + 36 ÷ 12 = 24 + 3 = **27** *(1 mark)*

6) $100 − 5^2 = 100 − 25 = $ **75** *(1 mark)*
   $10^2 + 10^3 = 100 + 1000 = $ **1100** *(1 mark)*

7) 45 − 100 = **−55** *(1 mark)*
   −85 + 92 = **7** *(1 mark)*

8) $(3^3 + 2) \times 10 = (27 + 2) \times 10 = 29 \times 10 = $ **290** *(1 mark)*
   $2 \times 70 − 8^2 = 140 − 64 = $ **76** *(1 mark)*

Section Two — Calculations

Pages 10-12 — Written Addition

1) 26 + 4 = 30, so 126 + 504 = **630** *(1 mark)*
   97 + 3 = 100, so 497 + 203 = **700** *(1 mark)*

2)
   ```
     452        7041
   + 241      + 357
    ―――       ――――
     693       7398
   ```
   (1 mark for each correct answer)

3) **784** = 33 + 751 *(1 mark)*
   876 = 571 + 305 *(1 mark)*
   968 = 686 + 282 *(1 mark)*

4)
   ```
     986        8736
   + 745      +  637
    ――――      ――――
    1731       9373
     1 1         1 1
   ```
   (1 mark for each correct answer)

5) 2305 + 3416 = **5721** *(1 mark)*
   5933 + 1325 = **7258** *(1 mark)*
   8542 + 7235 = **15 777** *(1 mark)*

6)
   ```
     3823      49285
   + 1299    +  1631
    ――――     ―――――
     5122     50916
    1 1 1      1  1
   ```
   (1 mark for each correct answer)

7)
   ```
     8300
   +68700
    ―――――
    77000    (1 mark)
    1  1
   ```

8)
   ```
    36752      54906
   + 6285    +81347
    ―――――     ―――――
    43037     136253
     1 1 1     1 1 1
   ```
   (1 mark for each correct answer)

9)
   ```
    759218
   + 85945
    ―――――――
    845163    (1 mark)
     1 1 1 1
   ```

Answers

Pages 13-15 — Written Subtraction

1) 458 − 101 = **357** *(1 mark)*
   715 − 306 = **409** *(1 mark)*
   1672 − 49 = **1623** *(1 mark)*

2) 4000 − 30 = **3970** *(1 mark)*
   70 000 − 600 = **69 400** *(1 mark)*

3)
   ```
     ⁶7³⁵                 ¹2⁵⁸14
   −  268              −    943
      467                  1671
   ```
   (1 mark for each correct answer)

4) **33** = 357 − 324 *(1 mark)*
   8 − 3 = 5 and 52 − 8 = 44,
   so **445** = 528 − 83 *(1 mark)*
   71 − 12 = 59,
   so **259** = 671 − 412 *(1 mark)*

5) Subtracting 185 from 822 gives the missing number:
   ```
     ⁷8²¹²
   −  185
      637   (1 mark)
   ```

6)
   ```
     ⁷8²8⁷4               ⁸9⁰9¹8¹1
   − 1348              −   2799
     6936                  6292
   ```
   (1 mark for each correct answer)

7) Subtracting 237 from 64 110 gives the missing number:
   ```
     6⁴4¹⁰1⁰10
   −      237
       63873    (1 mark)
   ```

8)
   ```
     ⁶7²3⁵59              ³4⁵6⁵4¹8⁷5
   − 28667             −  26898
     43892                19587
   ```
   (1 mark for each correct answer)

9)
   ```
     ⁸9⁰9¹0⁹1⁴5
   −    89152
       819993   (1 mark)
   ```

Pages 16-17 — Multiplying and Dividing by 10, 100 and 1000

1) 41 × 10 = **410** *(1 mark)*
   57 × 100 = **5700** *(1 mark)*

2) 80 ÷ 10 = **8** *(1 mark)*
   300 ÷ 100 = **3** *(1 mark)*

3) 676 × 100 = **67 600** *(1 mark)*
   93 × 10 × 10 = **9300** *(1 mark)*
   5 × 10 × 100 = **5000** *(1 mark)*

4) 500 ÷ 10 = **50** *(1 mark)*
   72 000 ÷ 10 = **7200** *(1 mark)*

5) 36 × 1000 = **36 000** *(1 mark)*
   8000 ÷ 1000 = **8** *(1 mark)*

6) 535 × 1000 = **535 000** *(1 mark)*
   2793 × 100 = **279 300** *(1 mark)*

7) 38 000 ÷ 1000 = **38** *(1 mark)*
   60 000 ÷ 1000 = **60** *(1 mark)*

8) 4900 ÷ **10** = 490 *(1 mark)*
   57 × 1000 = 57 000, so
   57 × 10 × **100** = 57 000 *(1 mark)*

Pages 18-19 — Using Times Tables

1) 7 × 9 = **63** *(1 mark)*
   11 × 12 = **132** *(1 mark)*

2) 32 ÷ 8 = **4** *(1 mark)*
   84 ÷ 7 = **12** *(1 mark)*

3) 6 × **7** = 42 *(1 mark)*
   121 ÷ **11** = 11 *(1 mark)*

4) 2 × 3 × 9 = 6 × 9 = **54** *(1 mark)*
   4 × 5 × 10 = 20 × 10 = **200** *(1 mark)*

5) 81 × **0** = 0 *(1 mark)*
   27 ÷ **1** = 27 *(1 mark)*

6) 50 × 60 = **3000** *(1 mark)*
   80 × 30 = **2400** *(1 mark)*

7) 350 ÷ 7 = **50** *(1 mark)*
   490 ÷ 70 = **7** *(1 mark)*

8) 4 × 3 × 60 = 12 × 60 = **720** *(1 mark)*
   20 × 30 × 8 = 600 × 8 = **4800** *(1 mark)*

Pages 20-23 — Written Multiplication

1)
   ```
      52           34
   ×   4        ×   3
     208          102
   ```
   (1 mark for each correct answer)

2)
   ```
      28           49
   ×   5        ×   7
     140          343
   ```
   (1 mark for each correct answer)

3)
   ```
     226          306
   ×   3        ×   8
     678         2448
   ```
   (1 mark for each correct answer)

4)
   ```
     495          798
   ×   6        ×   9
    2970         7182
   ```
   (1 mark for each correct answer)

5)
   ```
    1071         2489
   ×    5      ×    3
    5355         7467
   ```
   (1 mark for each correct answer)

6)
   ```
      23
   ×  13
      69
     230
     299
   ```
   (2 marks for the correct answer, or 1 mark for long multiplication with no more than one error)

   ```
      31
   ×  16
     186
     310
     496
   ```
   (2 marks for the correct answer, or 1 mark for long multiplication with no more than one error)

7)
   ```
      68
   ×  25
     340
    1360
    1700
   ```
   (2 marks for the correct answer, or 1 mark for long multiplication with no more than one error)

   ```
      79
   ×  46
     474
    3160
    3634
   ```
   (2 marks for the correct answer, or 1 mark for long multiplication with no more than one error)

8)
   ```
     203
   ×  22
     406
    4060
    4466
   ```
   (2 marks for the correct answer, or 1 mark for long multiplication with no more than one error)

   ```
     112
   ×  94
     448
   10080
   10528
   ```
   (2 marks for the correct answer, or 1 mark for long multiplication with no more than one error)

Answers

$$\begin{array}{r} 866 \\ \times\ 53 \\ \hline 2\,5\,9\,8 \\ 4\,3\,3\,0\,0 \\ \hline \underline{45898} \end{array}$$

(2 marks for the correct answer, or 1 mark for long multiplication with no more than one error)

$$\begin{array}{r} 492 \\ \times\ 47 \\ \hline 3\,4\,4\,4 \\ 1\,9\,6\,8\,0 \\ \hline \underline{23124} \end{array}$$

(2 marks for the correct answer, or 1 mark for long multiplication with no more than one error)

9)
$$\begin{array}{r} 8411 \\ \times\ 21 \\ \hline 8411 \\ 16\,8220 \\ \hline \underline{176631} \end{array}$$

(2 marks for the correct answer, or 1 mark for long multiplication with no more than one error)

$$\begin{array}{r} 2707 \\ \times\ 15 \\ \hline 1\,3\,5\,3\,5 \\ 2\,7\,0\,7\,0 \\ \hline \underline{40605} \end{array}$$

(2 marks for the correct answer, or 1 mark for long multiplication with no more than one error)

$$\begin{array}{r} 3291 \\ \times\ 54 \\ \hline 1\,3\,1\,6\,4 \\ 1\,6\,4\,5\,5\,0 \\ \hline \underline{177714} \end{array}$$

(2 marks for the correct answer, or 1 mark for long multiplication with no more than one error)

$$\begin{array}{r} 7426 \\ \times\ 46 \\ \hline 4\,4\,5\,5\,6 \\ 2\,9\,7\,0\,4\,0 \\ \hline \underline{341596} \end{array}$$

(2 marks for the correct answer, or 1 mark for long multiplication with no more than one error)

10)
$$\begin{array}{r} 8365 \\ \times\ 79 \\ \hline 7\,5\,2\,8\,5 \\ 5\,8\,5\,5\,5\,0 \\ \hline \underline{660835} \end{array}$$

(2 marks for the correct answer, or 1 mark for long multiplication with no more than one error)

Pages 24-27 — Written Division

1) $3\overline{)7\,^{1}2} = 24$ $7\overline{)9\,^{2}8} = 14$
   (1 mark for each correct answer)

2) $4\overline{)4\,3\,^{3}6} = 109$ $6\overline{)5\,5\,^{1}8} = 93$
   (1 mark for each correct answer)

3) $8\overline{)8\,9\,^{1}6\,8} = 1121$ $5\overline{)4\,^{4}2\,^{2}8\,^{3}5} = 857$
   (1 mark for each correct answer)

4) $3\overline{)7\,^{1}6} = 25\,r1$ $9\overline{)2\,^{2}9\,^{2}1} = 32\,r3$
   (1 mark for each correct answer)

5) $6\overline{)9\,^{3}7\,^{1}0\,^{4}4} = 1617\,r2$ *(1 mark)*

   $8\overline{)4\,^{4}1\,^{1}9\,^{3}9} = 524\,r7$ *(1 mark)*

6)
$$\begin{array}{r} 15 \\ 13\overline{)195} \\ -\underline{13} \\ 65 \\ -\underline{65} \\ 0 \end{array}$$

(2 marks for the correct answer, or 1 mark for a written method with no more than one error)

$$\begin{array}{r} 12 \\ 21\overline{)252} \\ -\underline{21} \\ 42 \\ -\underline{42} \\ 0 \end{array}$$

(2 marks for the correct answer, or 1 mark for a written method with no more than one error)

7)
$$\begin{array}{r} 22 \\ 24\overline{)528} \\ -\underline{48} \\ 48 \\ -\underline{48} \\ 0 \end{array}$$

(2 marks for the correct answer, or 1 mark for a written method with no more than one error)

$$\begin{array}{r} 25 \\ 33\overline{)825} \\ -\underline{66} \\ 165 \\ -\underline{165} \\ 0 \end{array}$$
$33 \times 5 = 150 + 15 = 165$

(2 marks for the correct answer, or 1 mark for a written method with no more than one error)

8)
$$\begin{array}{r} 122 \\ 43\overline{)5246} \\ -\underline{43} \\ 94 \\ -\underline{86} \\ 86 \\ -\underline{86} \\ 0 \end{array}$$

(2 marks for the correct answer, or 1 mark for a written method with no more than one error)

$$\begin{array}{r} 124 \\ 74\overline{)9176} \\ -\underline{74} \\ 177 \\ -\underline{148} \\ 296 \\ -\underline{296} \\ 0 \end{array}$$
$74 \times 4 = 280 + 16 = 296$

(2 marks for the correct answer, or 1 mark for a written method with no more than one error)

$$\begin{array}{r} 94 \\ 52\overline{)4888} \\ -\underline{468} \\ 208 \\ -\underline{208} \\ 0 \end{array}$$
$52 \times 9 = 520 - 52 = 468$

(2 marks for the correct answer, or 1 mark for a written method with no more than one error)

$$\begin{array}{r} 95 \\ 39\overline{)3705} \\ -\underline{351} \\ 195 \\ -\underline{195} \\ 0 \end{array}$$
$39 \times 9 = 390 - 39 = 351$
$39 \times 5 = 150 + 45 = 195$

(2 marks for the correct answer, or 1 mark for a written method with no more than one error)

9)
$$\begin{array}{r} 23\,r9 \\ 23\overline{)538} \\ -\underline{46} \\ 78 \\ -\underline{69} \\ 9 \end{array}$$

(2 marks for the correct answer, or 1 mark for a written method with no more than one error)

$$\begin{array}{r} 14\,r20 \\ 61\overline{)874} \\ -\underline{61} \\ 264 \\ -\underline{244} \\ 20 \end{array}$$
$61 \times 4 = 240 + 4 = 244$

(2 marks for the correct answer, or 1 mark for a written method with no more than one error)

© CGP — Not to be photocopied

Answers

10)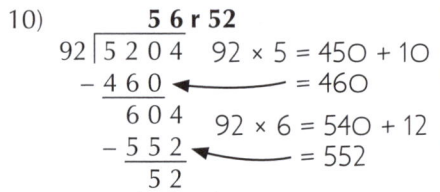
```
      5 6 r 52
92 ) 5 2 0 4      92 × 5 = 450 + 10
   − 4 6 0              = 460
     6 0 4        92 × 6 = 540 + 12
   −  5 5 2             = 552
         5 2
```
(2 marks for the correct answer, or 1 mark for a written method with no more than one error)

```
      1 2 6 r 31
77 ) 9 7 3 3
   −  7 7       77 × 2 = 140 + 14
     2 0 3            = 154
   − 1 5 4
     4 9 3      77 × 6 = 420 + 42
   − 4 6 2            = 462
       3 1
```
(2 marks for the correct answer, or 1 mark for a written method with no more than one error)

Pages 28-29 — Mixed Practice

1) 54 × 100 = **5400** *(1 mark)*
   604 × 1000 = **604 000** *(1 mark)*
   7800 ÷ 10 = **780** *(1 mark)*
   42 000 ÷ 100 = **420** *(1 mark)*

2) **1300** = 881 + 419 *(1 mark)*
   96 − 78 = 18,
   so **418** = 796 − 378 *(1 mark)*
   83 − 25 = 58,
   so 9831 − **9580** = 251 *(1 mark)*

3) 3 × 3 × 8 = 9 × 8 = **72** *(1 mark)*
   50 × 2 × 4 = 100 × 4 = **400**
   (1 mark)

4)
```
      9 1 7
4 ) 3 ³6 6 ²8    (1 mark)

     9 0 3 6
   ×     7
     6 3 2 5 2   (1 mark)
         ₂ ₄
```

5)
```
    7 9 3 5 6 8
  +   2 7 3 8 4
    8 2 0 9 5 2    (1 mark)
    ₁ ₁   ₁ ₁

    ⁴9̷ ¹2 ¹5 ¹0
    5̷ 0̷ 3̷ 6̷ ¹4
  −    8 4 7 8 9
    4 1 8 8 2 5    (1 mark)
```

6)
```
       9 7 2 3
   ×      8 4
     3 8 ₈9 ₁2
   7 7 ₁7 ₁8 4 0
   8 1 6 7 3 2
   ₁ ₁   ₁ ₁
```
(2 marks for the correct answer, or 1 mark for long multiplication with no more than one error)

```
     9 2
67 ) 6 1 6 4     67 × 9 = 670 − 67
   − 6 0 3             = 603
     1 3 4       67 × 2 = 120 + 14
   − 1 3 4             = 134
         0
```
(2 marks for the correct answer, or 1 mark for a written method with no more than one error)

Section Three — Decimals
Pages 30-31 — Adding and Subtracting Decimals

1)
```
    4.3         7.6
  + 5.6       − 0.2
    9.9         7.4

    3 5.8       6⁸9̷.¹4
  +   2.5     −   4.7
    3 8.3       6 4.7
        ₁
```
(1 mark for each correct answer)

2)
```
      2.8 6         ²5̷.⁰9
   +  3.6 1       −   1.3 4
      6.4 7         2 3.7 5
      ₁
```
(1 mark for each correct answer)

3)
```
    1 1 6.7 4       ⁷8̷.¹2 7
  +   4 2.4 0     −   5.4 0
    1 5 9.1 4         2.8 7
            ₁
```
(1 mark for each correct answer)

4)
```
    ⁰1̷ ¹2.⁵6̷ ¹4 1        6.3 0 0
   −    4.3 9 0       + 7.8 4 2
        8.2 5 1       1 4.1 4 2
                              ₁
```
(1 mark for each correct answer)

5)
```
    ⁷8̷.⁰0        ²3̷ ¹3⁴.³0
  − 2.7       − 1 6.5 2
    5.3         1 7.7 8
```
(1 mark for each correct answer)

6)
```
    3 2 6.5 2        ¹2̷ ²3̷.⁵6̷ ⁹0̷ ¹0
  +   7 4.9 0      −      7.8 1 4
    4 0 1.4 2        1 5.7 8 6
    ₁ ₁   ₁
```
(1 mark for each correct answer)

Pages 32-33 — Multiplying and Dividing by 10, 100 and 1000

1) 13.2 × 10 = **132** *(1 mark)*
   9.431 × 10 = **94.31** *(1 mark)*
   204.78 × 10 = **2047.8** *(1 mark)*

2) 3.15 × 100 = **315** *(1 mark)*
   62.8 × 100 = **6280** *(1 mark)*

3) 4.87 × 1000 = **4870** *(1 mark)*
   6.935 × 1000 = **6935** *(1 mark)*
   124.3 × 1000 = **124 300** *(1 mark)*

4) 0.8 ÷ 10 = **0.08** *(1 mark)*
   1.63 ÷ 10 = **0.163** *(1 mark)*

5) 0.6 ÷ 100 = **0.006** *(1 mark)*
   17 ÷ 100 = **0.17** *(1 mark)*
   2.8 ÷ 100 = **0.028** *(1 mark)*
   24.6 ÷ 100 = **0.246** *(1 mark)*

6) 349 ÷ 1000 = **0.349** *(1 mark)*
   12 ÷ 1000 = **0.012** *(1 mark)*

7) 7.486 × **100** = 748.6 *(1 mark)*
   0.1 ÷ 10 = 0.01 *(1 mark)*
   3075 ÷ **1000** = 3.075 *(1 mark)*

Pages 34-35 — Multiplying with Decimals

1) 5 × 6 = 30, so
   0.5 × 6 = 30 ÷ 10 = **3** *(1 mark)*
   4 × 9 = 36, so
   0.04 × 9 = 36 ÷ 100
            = **0.36** *(1 mark)*
   3 × 8 = 24, so
   3 × 0.08 = 24 ÷ 100
            = **0.24** *(1 mark)*
   11 × 7 = 77, so
   11 × 0.7 = 77 ÷ 10
            = **7.7** *(1 mark)*

2) 6 × 80 = 6 × 8 × 10 = 480,
   so 0.6 × 80 = 480 ÷ 10
              = **48** *(1 mark)*
   2 × 50 = 100,
   so 0.02 × 50 = 100 ÷ 100
                = **1** *(1 mark)*
   300 × 7 = 3 × 7 × 100 = 2100,
   so 300 × 0.07 = 2100 ÷ 100
                 = **21** *(1 mark)*

3)
```
      5 2
   ×   4
     2 0 8
```
   So 5.2 × 4 = 208 ÷ 10
             = **20.8** *(1 mark)*
```
      2 7
   ×   8
     2 1 6
       ₅
```
   So 27 × 0.8 = 216 ÷ 10
              = **21.6** *(1 mark)*

4)
```
      3 5
   ×   6
     2 1 0
       ₃
```
   So 0.06 × 35 = 210 ÷ 100
               = **2.1** *(1 mark)*

Answers

$$\begin{array}{r} 641 \\ \times\ \ \ 7 \\ \hline 4487 \\ _2\ \ \ \end{array}$$
So 6.41 × 7 = 4487 ÷ 100
= **44.87** *(1 mark)*

5) $$\begin{array}{r} 29 \\ \times\ \ 4 \\ \hline 116 \\ _3\ \ \end{array}$$
So 29 × 40 = 1160.
2.9 × 40 = 1160 ÷ 10
= **116** *(1 mark)*

$$\begin{array}{r} 537 \\ \times\ \ \ 5 \\ \hline 2685 \\ _{1\ 3}\ \end{array}$$
So 537 × 50 = 26 850.
5.37 × 50 = 26 850 ÷ 100
= **268.5** *(1 mark)*

6) $$\begin{array}{r} 34 \\ \times 15 \\ \hline 17_20 \\ 340 \\ \hline 510 \\ _1\ \ \ \end{array}$$
So 3.4 × 15 = 510 ÷ 10 = **51**
(2 marks for the correct answer, or 1 mark for working with no more than one error)

$$\begin{array}{r} 25 \\ \times\ \ 92 \\ \hline 5_10 \\ 22_450 \\ \hline 2300 \\ _1\ \ \ \ \end{array}$$
So 25 × 9.2 = 2300 ÷ 10 = **230**
(2 marks for the correct answer, or 1 mark for working with no more than one error)

Pages 36-37 — Dividing with Decimals

1) 8 ÷ 4 = 2, so
0.8 ÷ 4 = 2 ÷ 10 = **0.2** *(1 mark)*
32 ÷ 8 = 4, so
3.2 ÷ 8 = 4 ÷ 10 = **0.4** *(1 mark)*
56 ÷ 7 = 8, so
0.56 ÷ 7 = 8 ÷ 100
= **0.08** *(1 mark)*
84 ÷ 12 = 7, so
8.4 ÷ 12 = 7 ÷ 10
= **0.7** *(1 mark)*

2) 69 ÷ 3 = 23, so
6.9 ÷ 3 = 23 ÷ 10 = **2.3** *(1 mark)*
482 ÷ 2 = 241, so
4.82 ÷ 2 = 241 ÷ 100
= **2.41** *(1 mark)*

155 ÷ 5 = 31, so
15.5 ÷ 5 = 31 ÷ 10
= **3.1** *(1 mark)*

3) $$\begin{array}{r} 32 \\ 8\overline{)2\,^25\,^16} \end{array}$$
So 25.6 ÷ 8 = 32 ÷ 10
= **3.2** *(1 mark)*

$$\begin{array}{r} 27 \\ 4\overline{)1\,1^20\,^28} \end{array}$$
So 1.08 ÷ 4 = 27 ÷ 100
= **0.27** *(1 mark)*

4) 12 ÷ 5 = 2 remainder 2
= $2\frac{2}{5}$ = **2.4** *(1 mark)*

43 ÷ 4 = 10 remainder 3
= $10\frac{3}{4}$ = **10.75** *(1 mark)*

5) $$\begin{array}{r} 26.5 \\ 6\overline{)1\,^15\,^39.^30} \end{array}$$ *(1 mark)*

$$\begin{array}{r} 53.25 \\ 8\overline{)4\,^42\,^26.^20\,^40} \end{array}$$ *(1 mark)*

6) $$\begin{array}{r} 21.5 \\ 22\overline{)473.0} \\ -44 \\ \hline 33 \\ -22 \\ \hline 110 \\ -110 \\ \hline 0 \end{array}$$
(2 marks for the correct answer, or 1 mark for a written method with no more than one error)

$$\begin{array}{r} 434.5 \\ 12\overline{)5214.0} \\ -48 \\ \hline 41 \\ -36 \\ \hline 54 \\ -48 \\ \hline 60 \\ -60 \\ \hline 0 \end{array}$$
(2 marks for the correct answer, or 1 mark for a written method with no more than one error)

Pages 38-39 — Mixed Practice

1) $$\begin{array}{r} 4.19 \\ +3.25 \\ \hline 7.44 \\ _1\ \ \ \end{array}\quad\begin{array}{r} 7.530 \\ +2.648 \\ \hline 10.178 \\ _1\ \ \ \ \ \end{array}$$
(1 mark for each correct answer)

2) 8.97 × 10 = **89.7** *(1 mark)*
0.62 × 1000 = **620** *(1 mark)*
0.3 ÷ 100 = **0.003** *(1 mark)*
58 ÷ 1000 = **0.058** *(1 mark)*

3) $$\begin{array}{r} ^1\!2^{14}\!3.^1\!3 \\ -16.7 \\ \hline 8.6 \end{array}\quad\begin{array}{r} ^8\!\cancel{9}.^9\!\cancel{0}\,^1\!0 \\ -7.29 \\ \hline 1.71 \end{array}$$
(1 mark for each correct answer)

4) 5 × 7 = 35, so
0.05 × 7 = 35 ÷ 100
= **0.35** *(1 mark)*
36 ÷ 9 = 4, so
0.36 ÷ 9 = 4 ÷ 100
= **0.04** *(1 mark)*

5) $$\begin{array}{r} 842 \\ \times\ \ \ 5 \\ \hline 4210 \\ _{2\ 1}\ \end{array}$$
So 8.42 × 5 = 4210 ÷ 100
= **42.1** *(1 mark)*

$$\begin{array}{r} 44 \\ \times\ \ 54 \\ \hline 17_66 \\ 22_200 \\ \hline 2376 \end{array}$$
So 44 × 5.4 = 2376 ÷ 10 = **237.6**
(2 marks for the correct answer, or 1 mark for working with no more than one error)

6) $$\begin{array}{r} 63 \\ 6\overline{)3\,^37\,^18} \end{array}$$
So 3.78 ÷ 6 = 63 ÷ 100
= **0.63** *(1 mark)*

$$\begin{array}{r} 23.5 \\ 14\overline{)329.0} \\ -28 \\ \hline 49 \\ -42 \\ \hline 70 \\ -70 \\ \hline 0 \end{array}$$
(2 marks for the correct answer, or 1 mark for a written method with no more than one error)

Section Four — Fractions

Pages 40-42 — Adding and Subtracting Fractions

1) $\frac{3}{7} + \frac{2}{7} = \frac{3+2}{7} = \frac{5}{7}$ *(1 mark)*
$\frac{5}{8} + \frac{4}{8} = \frac{5+4}{8} = \frac{9}{8}$ or $1\frac{1}{8}$
(1 mark)

2) $\frac{7}{9} - \frac{1}{9} = \frac{7-1}{9} = \frac{6}{9}$ or $\frac{2}{3}$
(1 mark)
$\frac{9}{12} - \frac{5}{12} = \frac{9-5}{12} = \frac{4}{12}$ or $\frac{1}{3}$
(1 mark)

Answers

3) $\frac{4}{5} + \frac{2}{15} = \frac{12}{15} + \frac{2}{15} = \frac{14}{15}$
   (1 mark)

   $\frac{1}{2} - \frac{1}{6} = \frac{3}{6} - \frac{1}{6} = \frac{2}{6}$ or $\frac{1}{3}$
   (1 mark)

   $\frac{5}{6} + \frac{8}{9} = \frac{15}{18} + \frac{16}{18}$
   $= \frac{31}{18}$ or $1\frac{13}{18}$ *(1 mark)*

   $\frac{11}{16} - \frac{3}{12} = \frac{11}{16} - \frac{4}{16} = \frac{7}{16}$
   (1 mark)

4) $1\frac{2}{5} + \frac{3}{5} = 1 + \frac{5}{5} = 2$ *(1 mark)*

   $1\frac{1}{10} - \frac{3}{10} = \frac{11}{10} - \frac{3}{10}$
   $= \frac{8}{10}$ or $\frac{4}{5}$ *(1 mark)*

5) $\frac{2}{11} + \frac{5}{11} + \frac{1}{11} = \frac{8}{11}$ *(1 mark)*

   $\frac{5}{14} + \frac{1}{7} + \frac{2}{14} = \frac{5}{14} + \frac{2}{14} + \frac{2}{14}$
   $= \frac{9}{14}$ *(1 mark)*

6) $\frac{3}{5} + \frac{1}{4} = \frac{12}{20} + \frac{5}{20} = \frac{17}{20}$
   (1 mark)

   $\frac{2}{6} + \frac{2}{7} = \frac{14}{42} + \frac{12}{42}$
   $= \frac{26}{42}$ or $\frac{13}{21}$ *(1 mark)*

   $\frac{9}{10} - \frac{2}{3} = \frac{27}{30} - \frac{20}{30} = \frac{7}{30}$
   (1 mark)

   $\frac{6}{11} - \frac{1}{2} = \frac{12}{22} - \frac{11}{22} = \frac{1}{22}$
   (1 mark)

7) $5\frac{3}{8} + \frac{3}{4} = 5 + \frac{3}{8} + \frac{6}{8}$
   $= 5 + \frac{9}{8} = 5 + 1\frac{1}{8}$
   $= 6\frac{1}{8}$ or $\frac{49}{8}$ *(1 mark)*

   $2\frac{2}{3} - \frac{4}{5} = \frac{8}{3} - \frac{4}{5} = \frac{40}{15} - \frac{12}{15}$
   $= \frac{28}{15}$ or $1\frac{13}{15}$ *(1 mark)*

8) $1\frac{1}{4} + 1\frac{1}{3} = 1 + 1 + \frac{3}{12} + \frac{4}{12}$
   $= 2\frac{7}{12}$ or $\frac{31}{12}$
   (1 mark)

   $2\frac{1}{6} - 1\frac{2}{5} = \frac{13}{6} - \frac{7}{5}$
   $= \frac{65}{30} - \frac{42}{30} = \frac{23}{30}$ *(1 mark)*

Pages 43-44 — Multiplying Fractions

1) $\frac{1}{4}$ of $400 = 400 \div 4$
   $= 100$ *(1 mark)*

   $\frac{1}{5}$ of $1000 = 1000 \div 5 = 200$,
   so $\frac{2}{5}$ of $1000 = 2 \times 200$
   $= 400$ *(1 mark)*

2) $\frac{1}{9} \times 270 = 270 \div 9$
   $= 30$ *(1 mark)*

   $\frac{1}{6} \times 6600 = 6600 \div 6$
   $= 1100$ *(1 mark)*

3) $14 \div 7 = 2$, $5 \times 2 = 10$
   So $\frac{5}{7} \times 14 = 10$ *(1 mark)*

   $200 \div 100 = 2$, $51 \times 2 = 102$
   So $\frac{51}{100} \times 200 = 102$ *(1 mark)*

4) $210 \div 3 = 70$, $2 \times 70 = 140$
   So $\frac{2}{3}$ of $210 = 140$ *(1 mark)*

   $30 \div 4 = 7.5$, $3 \times 7.5 = 22.5$
   So $\frac{3}{4}$ of $30 = 22.5$ *(1 mark)*

5) $\frac{1}{2} \times 32 = 32 \div 2 = 16$
   $1\frac{1}{2} \times 32 = 32 + 16$
   $= 48$ *(1 mark)*

   $125 \div 5 = 25$, $2 \times 25 = 50$
   So $\frac{2}{5}$ of $125 = 50$
   $1\frac{2}{5} \times 125 = 125 + 50$
   $= 175$ *(1 mark)*

6) $\frac{1}{5} \times \frac{1}{11} = \frac{1 \times 1}{5 \times 11} = \frac{1}{55}$
   (1 mark)

   $\frac{1}{2} \times \frac{3}{8} = \frac{1 \times 3}{2 \times 8} = \frac{3}{16}$ *(1 mark)*

   $\frac{9}{10} \times \frac{2}{3} = \frac{9 \times 2}{10 \times 3} = \frac{18}{30}$ or $\frac{3}{5}$
   (1 mark)

   $\frac{3}{4} \times \frac{2}{15} = \frac{3 \times 2}{4 \times 15} = \frac{6}{60}$ or $\frac{1}{10}$
   (1 mark)

Page 45 — Dividing Fractions

1) $\frac{7}{10} \div 7 = \frac{7 \div 7}{10} = \frac{1}{10}$ *(1 mark)*

   $\frac{2}{3} \div 2 = \frac{2 \div 2}{3} = \frac{1}{3}$

   $\frac{8}{13} \div 4 = \frac{8 \div 4}{13} = \frac{2}{13}$

   $\frac{20}{75} \div 10 = \frac{20 \div 10}{75} = \frac{2}{75}$
   (1 mark)

2) $\frac{1}{3} \div 4 = \frac{1}{3 \times 4} = \frac{1}{12}$ *(1 mark)*

   $\frac{1}{6} \div 10 = \frac{1}{6 \times 10} = \frac{1}{60}$ *(1 mark)*

   $\frac{3}{8} \div 5 = \frac{3}{8 \times 5} = \frac{3}{40}$ *(1 mark)*

   $\frac{2}{7} \div 4 = \frac{2}{7 \times 4} = \frac{2}{28}$ or $\frac{1}{14}$
   (1 mark)

Pages 46-47 — Percentages

1) 10% of $500 = 500 \div 10$
   $= 50$ *(1 mark)*

   25% of $4000 = 4000 \div 4$
   $= 1000$ *(1 mark)*

   50% of $840 = 840 \div 2$
   $= 420$ *(1 mark)*

   1% of $1000 = 1000 \div 100$
   $= 10$ *(1 mark)*

2) 10% of $120 = 120 \div 10 = 12$
   20% of $120 = 2 \times 12$
   $= 24$ *(1 mark)*

   10% of $3600 = 3600 \div 10 = 360$
   50% of $3600 = 3600 \div 2 = 1800$
   60% of $3600 = 1800 + 360$
   $= 2160$ *(1 mark)*

   10% of $940 = 940 \div 10 = 94$
   5% of $940 = 94 \div 2 = 47$
   15% of $940 = 94 + 47$
   $= 141$ *(1 mark)*

   50% of $280 = 280 \div 2 = 140$
   10% of $280 = 280 \div 10 = 28$
   5% of $280 = 28 \div 2 = 14$
   65% of $280 = 140 + 28 + 14$
   $= 182$ *(1 mark)*

3) 10% × $10\,000 = 10\,000 \div 10$
   $= 1000$
   40% × $10\,000 = 1000 \times 4$
   $= 4000$ *(1 mark)*

   10% × $160 = 160 \div 10 = 16$
   5% × $160 = 16 \div 2 = 8$
   35% × $160 = 3 \times 16 + 8$
   $= 56$ *(1 mark)*

4) 1% of $4500 = 4500 \div 100 = 45$
   99% of $4500 = 4500 - 45$
   $= 4455$ *(1 mark)*

   50% of $700 = 700 \div 2 = 350$
   1% of $700 = 700 \div 100 = 7$
   49% of $700 = 350 - 7$
   $= 343$ *(1 mark)*

   10% of $300 = 300 \div 10 = 30$
   1% of $300 = 300 \div 100 = 3$
   9% of $300 = 30 - 3 = 27$ *(1 mark)*

   25% of $600 = 600 \div 4 = 150$
   1% of $600 = 600 \div 100 = 6$
   26% of $600 = 150 + 6$
   $= 156$ *(1 mark)*

5) 50% of $1600 = 1600 \div 2 = 800$
   10% of $1600 = 1600 \div 10 = 160$
   5% of $1600 = 800 \div 10 = 80$
   1% of $1600 = 160 \div 10 = 16$
   67% of 1600
   $= 800 + 160 + 80 + 16 + 16$
   $= 1072$ *(1 mark)*

Answers

Pages 48–49 — Mixed Practice

1) 10% of 270 = 270 ÷ 10 = 27
   30% of 270 = 3 × 27
   = **81** (1 mark)
   10% of 5000 = 5000 ÷ 10 = 500
   90% of 5000 = 5000 − 500
   = **4500** (1 mark)

2) $\frac{1}{8}$ × 560 = 560 ÷ 8 = **70** (1 mark)
   450 ÷ 5 = 90, 2 × 90 = 180
   So $\frac{2}{5}$ × 450 = **180** (1 mark)

3) $\frac{1}{10} + \frac{2}{9} = \frac{9}{90} + \frac{20}{90} = \frac{29}{90}$
   (1 mark)
   $\frac{1}{2} - \frac{3}{7} = \frac{7}{14} - \frac{6}{14} = \frac{1}{14}$
   (1 mark)

4) 50% of 2800 = 2800 ÷ 2 = 1400
   1% of 2800 = 2800 ÷ 100 = 28
   52% of 2800 = 1400 + 28 + 28
   = **1456** (1 mark)

5) $\frac{4}{5} \div 10 = \frac{4}{5 \times 10} = \frac{4}{50}$ or $\frac{2}{25}$
   (1 mark)
   $\frac{1}{9} \div 3 = \frac{1}{9 \times 3} = \frac{1}{27}$ (1 mark)

6) $\frac{5}{6} \times \frac{4}{5} = \frac{5 \times 4}{6 \times 5} = \frac{20}{30}$ or $\frac{2}{3}$
   (1 mark)

7) $1\frac{3}{5} + \frac{2}{3} = 1 + \frac{9}{15} + \frac{10}{15}$
   $= 1 + \frac{19}{15} = 1 + 1\frac{4}{15}$
   $= 2\frac{4}{15}$ or $\frac{34}{15}$ (1 mark)
   $1\frac{5}{6} - \frac{9}{12}$
   $= \frac{11}{6} - \frac{9}{12} = \frac{22}{12} - \frac{9}{12}$
   $= \frac{13}{12}$ or $1\frac{1}{12}$ (1 mark)
   $\frac{1}{3} \times 90 = 90 \div 3 = 30$
   $1\frac{1}{3} \times 90 = 90 + 30$
   = **120** (1 mark)

Pages 50-54 — Practice Test

1) **6918** = 5918 + 1000 (1 mark)

2) $1\,{}^5\!6\,{}^1\!5\,3$
   − 2 6 2
   1 3 9 1 (1 mark)

3) **499** + 10 = 509 (1 mark)

4) 66 ÷ 6 = **11** (1 mark)

5) **0** = 675 × 0 (1 mark)

6) **2800** = 28 × 100 (1 mark)

7) 4 2 7 5
   + 3 7 6
   4 6 5 1 (1 mark)

8) 21 − 5 = 16 and 0.4 − 0.3 = 0.1,
   so 21.4 − 5.3 = **16.1** (1 mark)

9) 3 7
   × 6
   2 2 2 (1 mark)

10) 72 ÷ 12 = 6,
    so **60** = 720 ÷ 12 (1 mark)

11) 59 000 ÷ 100 = **590** (1 mark)

12) 8 2.5 0
    + 7.6 8
    9 0.1 8 (1 mark)

13) 302 178 = 300 000 + **2000** + 100 + 70 + 8 (1 mark)

14) $2\,{}^1\!3\,{}^{14}\!0\,{}^9\!4\,{}^1\!9$
    − 6 1 5 8
    1 8 8 9 1 (1 mark)

15) $\begin{array}{r} 4\,2 \\ 8\overline{)3\,{}^3\!3\,{}^1\!6} \end{array}$ $\begin{array}{r} 1\,2\,6 \\ 6\overline{)7\,{}^1\!5\,{}^3\!6} \end{array}$
    (1 mark for each correct answer)

16) $7^2 - 50 = 49 - 50 = -1$ (1 mark)

17) **4127** = 41.27 × 100 (1 mark)

18) $\frac{1}{3}$ of 9300 = 9300 ÷ 3
    = **3100** (1 mark)
    $\frac{3}{10}$ of 620: 620 ÷ 10 = 62,
    62 × 3 = **186**
    (1 mark)

19) $\frac{7}{12} + \frac{7}{8} = \frac{14}{24} + \frac{21}{24}$
    $= \frac{35}{24}$ or $1\frac{11}{24}$ (1 mark)

20) 40 × (50 + 20) = 40 × 70 = **2800**
    (1 mark)

21) 942 ÷ **1000** = 0.942 (1 mark)

22) $2\frac{1}{5} - 1\frac{5}{9} = \frac{11}{5} - \frac{14}{9}$
    $= \frac{99}{45} - \frac{70}{45}$
    $= \frac{29}{45}$ (1 mark)

23) 6 5 4
    × 3 4
    2 6${}_2$1${}_6$
    1 9${}_6$2 0
    2 2 2 3 6
    (2 marks for the correct answer, or 1 mark for long multiplication with no more than one error)

24) $\frac{16}{17} \div 4 = \frac{16 \div 4}{17} = \frac{4}{17}$ (1 mark)

25) $1\,{}^7\!8.{}^9\!0\,{}^9\!0\,{}^1\!0$
    − 7.9 2 6
    1 0.0 7 4 (1 mark)

26) 10% of 1200 = 1200 ÷ 10 = 120
    80% of 1200 = 8 × 120 = 960
    1% of 1200 = 1200 ÷ 100 = 12
    78% of 1200 = 960 − 12 − 12
    = **936** (1 mark)
    You could also have added 70% and 8%.

27) 4 × 7.2 = 4 × 7 + 4 × 0.2
    = 28 + 0.8
    = **28.8** (1 mark)
    5 × 34 = 5 × 30 + 5 × 4
    = 150 + 20 = 170
    So 50 × 3.4 = 170 × 10 ÷ 10
    = **170** (1 mark)

28) $\frac{19}{20} \div 3 = \frac{19}{20 \times 3}$
    $= \frac{19}{60}$ (1 mark)
    $\frac{3}{7} \times \frac{5}{8} = \frac{3 \times 5}{7 \times 8} = \frac{15}{56}$ (1 mark)

29) 18 ÷ 9 = 2, 7 × 2 = 14
    So $\frac{7}{9}$ × 18 = 14
    2 × 18 = 36
    $2\frac{7}{9}$ × 18 = 36 + 14 = **50** (1 mark)

30) $\begin{array}{r} 2\,3 \\ 34\overline{)7\,8\,2} \\ -\,6\,8 \\ \hline 1\,0\,2 \\ -\,1\,0\,2 \\ \hline 0 \end{array}$ 34 × 3 = 90 + 12
    = 102
    (2 marks for the correct answer, or 1 mark for a written method with no more than one error)

    $\begin{array}{r} 9\,3 \\ 56\overline{)5\,2\,0\,8} \\ -\,5\,0\,4 \\ \hline 1\,6\,8 \\ -\,1\,6\,8 \\ \hline 0 \end{array}$ 56 × 9 = 560 − 56
    = 504
    56 × 3 = 150 + 18
    = 168
    (2 marks for the correct answer, or 1 mark for a written method with no more than one error)

8 2 1 6
× 4 7
5 7${}_1$5${}_1$1${}_4$2
3 2 8 6${}_2$4 0
3 8 6 1 5 2
(2 marks for the correct answer, or 1 mark for long multiplication with no more than one error)

Progress Chart

Put your Mixed Practice scores in here and see how you've done.

Section One — Whole Numbers	/ 17
Section Two — Calculations	/ 17
Section Three — Decimals	/ 16
Section Four — Fractions	/ 13
Total	**/ 63**

See if you're on target by checking your marks in the table below.

0-31	You're not quite there yet, but don't worry. Look at the progress chart above and work out which are your weakest topics. Really focus on those bits — you'll improve your Arithmetic skills in no time.
32-50	Good job! You're doing well, but keep practising to make sure you're really ready for your test. If you spot certain Mixed Practice pages that you got a low mark in, go back and try that section again.
51-63	Well done — you've done brilliantly! Give yourself a huge pat on the back. Keep working hard and you'll be an Arithmetic star.

Had a go at all the topics? Now try doing the Practice Test at the back of the book.

Practice Test	/ 40

0-19	You might need to do a bit more practice, but don't panic — try the questions again until you know everything inside-out.
20-31	Well done — you've done a good job! Make sure you practise your weaker topics and you'll be on track for a great score.
32-40	You're a whizz at everything Arithmetic — congratulations!

This page may be photocopied